D0989763

Animal Offspring

Robins and Their Chicks

by Linda Tagliaferro

Consulting Editor: Gail Saunders-Smith, Ph.D.
Consultant: Brete G. Griffin, Education Director
American Birding Association
Colorado Springs, Colorado

Capstone press
Mankato, Minnesota

Pebble Plus is published by Capstone Press
151 Good Counsel Drive, P.O. Box 669, Mankato, Minnesota 56002
http://www.capstonepress.com

1 2 3 4 5 6 09 08 07 06 05 04

Library of Congress Cataloging-in-Publication Data
Tagliaferro, Linda.
   Robins and their chicks/by Linda Tagliaferro.
   p. cm.—(Pebble plus: Animal offspring)
   Includes bibliographical references (p. 23) and index.
   Contents: Robins—Eggs—Chicks—Growing up—Watch robins grow.
   ISBN 0-7368-2389-1 (hardcover)
   1. Robins—Infancy—Juvenile literature. 2. Parental behavior in animals—Juvenile literature. [1. Robins.
2. Animals—Infancy. 3. Parental behavior in animals.] I. Title. II. Series.
QL696.P288T34 2004
598.8'42—dc21   2003008490

Editorial Credits
Sarah L. Schuette, editor; Kia Adams, series designer; Kelly Garvin and Deirdre Barton, photo researchers;
   Karen Risch, product planning editor

Photo Credits
Ann & Rob Simpson, 1
Bruce Coleman Inc./Bob & Clara Calhoun, 17; Jeff Foott, 20 (left); John Shaw, 10–11; Laura Riley, 21 (left);
   L. L. Rue, 9; R. Kopfle, 14–15; S. Nielsen, 6–7
Corbis/Ron Austing; Frank Lane Picture Agency, cover; Roy Morsch, 13
Dwight R. Kuhn, 19
Eda Rogers, 21 (right)
Erwin & Peggy Bauer, 4–5, 20 (right)
PhotoDisc Inc., cover (leaves)

Note to Parents and Teachers

The Animal Offspring series supports national science standards related to life science.
This book describes and illustrates robins and their chicks. The images support early
readers in understanding the text. The repetition of words and phrases helps early
readers learn new words. This book also introduces early readers to subject-specific
vocabulary words, which are defined in the Glossary section. Early readers may need
assistance to read some words and to use the Table of Contents, Glossary, Read More,
Internet Sites, and Index/Word List sections of the book.

Word Count: 121
Early-Intervention Level: 13

Table of Contents

Robins

Robins and their chicks
are birds. Robins have dark
gray bodies and red breasts.

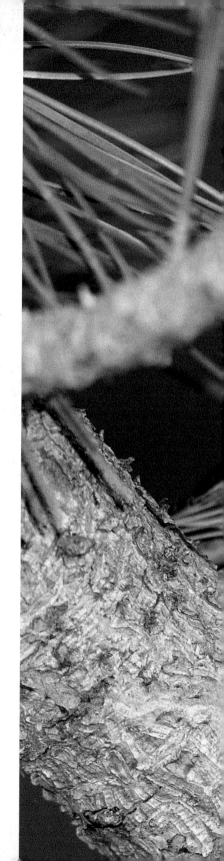

Female robins are hens.

Male robins are cocks.

Hens and cocks mate.

Then hens build nests.

Eggs

A hen lays three or four
blue eggs in the nest.

The hen sits on the eggs
to keep them warm.
She only leaves the nest
to look for food.

Chicks

Chicks hatch after 12 to 14 days. Newly hatched chicks have pink skin.

Robin parents leave the chicks to look for worms, insects, and berries.
The parents carry the food back to the nest.

Growing Up

The chicks reach to
get the food from
their parents.

Chicks use their wings when
they are about 13 days old.
Chicks become adults
after four months.

Watch Robins Grow

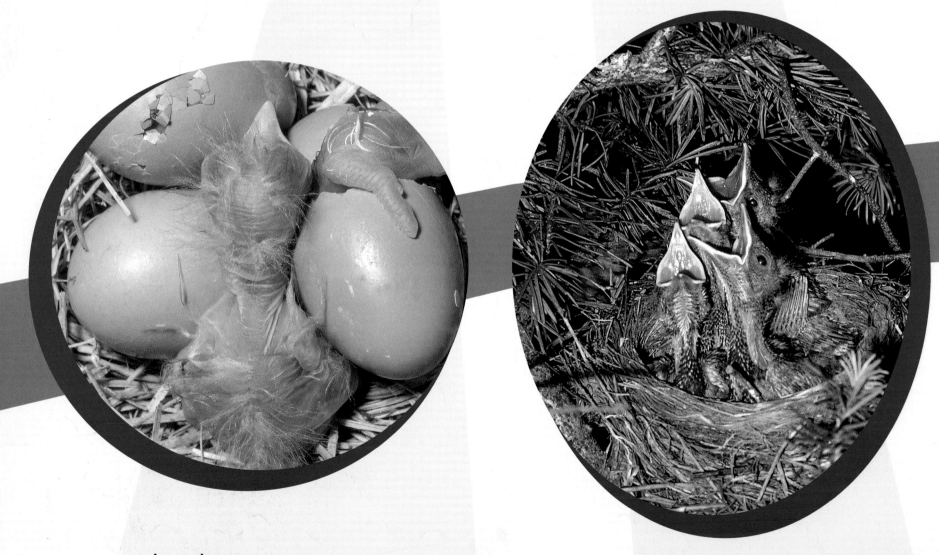

hatching

adult after about
four months

21

Glossary

adult—an animal that is able to mate

bird—a warm-blooded animal with wings, two legs, and feathers; most birds can fly.

breast—the front part of a robin's body; a male robin has brighter feathers on its breast than a female robin.

hatch—to break out of an egg

mate—to join together to produce young

nest—a place built to raise young; hens build nests out of dead grass, twigs, and mud.

Read More

Holmes, Anita. *Where Robins Fly*. We Can Read About Nature! New York: Benchmark Books, 2001.

Kottke, Jan. *From Egg to Robin*. How Things Grow. New York: Children's Press, 2000.

Posada, Mia. *Robins: Red Breasted Birds*. Minneapolis: Carolrhoda Books, 2004.

Internet Sites

FactHound offers a safe, fun way to find Internet sites related to this book. All of the sites on FactHound have been researched by our staff.

Here's how:

1. Visit *www.facthound.com*

2. Type in this special code **0736823891** for age-appropriate sites. Or enter a search word related to this book for a more general search.

3. Click on the Fetch It button.

FactHound will fetch the best sites for you!

Index/Word List